Plan of Nottingham, *c*.1902 .

BYGONE
NOTTINGHAM

A busy scene on Long Row (East), 1902.

BYGONE
NOTTINGHAM

Christopher Weir

Phillimore

1990

Published by
PHILLIMORE & CO. LTD.
Shopwyke Hall, Chichester, Sussex

ISBN 0 85033 745 3

Printed and bound in Great Britain by
BIDDLES LTD.
Guildford, Surrey

List of Illustrations

Frontispiece: Long Row (East), 1902

Acknowledgements

Nottinghamshire Local Studies Library: 1, 3, 5-7, 9-15, 17-21, 25, 28-31, 33, 35, 37-39, 42, 43, 45-47, 50-52, 56-60, 64, 65, 67, 72-80, 82-84, 87-95, 99, 100, 102, 105-107, 111-119, 122, 125-139, 142, 144, 145, 147, 149-153, 155, 156, 158, 162, 164; **Nottinghamshire Archives Office**: 2, 4, 16, 22-24, 26, 27, 32, 34, 36, 41, 44, 48, 49, 54, 55, 61, 63, 66, 68, 71, 81, 85, 86, 98, 104, 108-110, 121, 123, 124, 141, 143, 146, 148, 154, 157, 161, 163; **Private Collections**: 8, 53, 62, 96, 97, 140, 165; **York City Art Gallery**: 40; **Imperial Tobacco Limited**: 69, 70;**Raleigh Industries Limited**: 101, 159; **Author**: 103; **David S. Ackrel**: 120; ***Guardian Journal (Nottingham Evening Post)***: 160.

The author would like to thank the staff of the Nottinghamshire Local Studies Library, the Nottinghamshire Archives Office and the Brewhouse Yard Museum for their invaluable help and assistance. Copy photography was by John Birdsall and George L. Roberts.

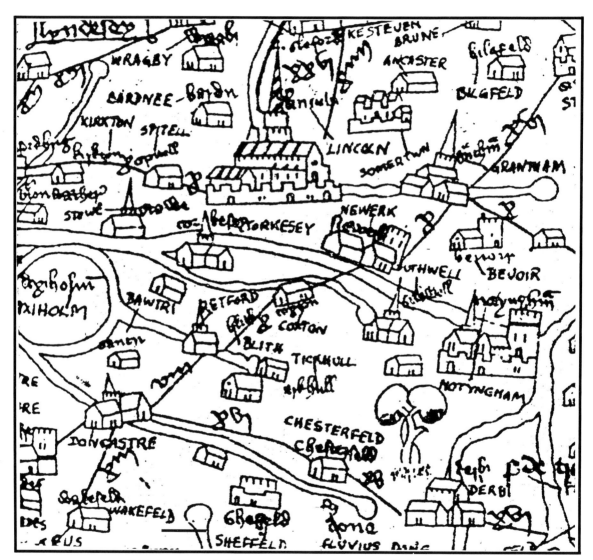

Nottinghamshire in the 14th century, from an early map in the Bodleian Library.

Introduction

Early Nottingham

The original Saxon borough of Nottingham stood on an elevated outcrop of sandstone overlooking the River Trent valley. The borough occupied a site of a little under forty acres, its boundary protected by a ditch and earthworks. In much later times the area covered by the Saxon borough became known as the Lace Market, and, though the defences have long since disappeared, the approximate course of the old borough boundary can still be traced. On the borough's western side the boundary ran between the parallel streets of Fletcher Gate and Bridlesmith Gate, while turning north the boundary is marked by Warser Gate and Woolpack Lane. The east side of the borough followed what is now Lower Parliament Street, with Hollowstone's sunken gap in the sandstone providing an almost certainly well guarded route in and out of the old borough. At the top of Hollowstone, alongside St Mary's church, the southern perimeter of the borough is followed by High Pavement, a long, curving street which ends at Weekday Cross, the site of the old borough's weekly market. From the south a steep sandstone cliff provided a formidable natural defence, and must have been an important factor in attracting early settlers to the site.

But the Saxon borough was to come under a new period of rule in the ninth century as Danish and Viking invaders finally overran the central Saxon kingdom of Mercia. Nottingham itself became part of the Danelaw, acquiring status as a military and trading town. A legacy of Danish influence can be found in the Scandinavian street-name ending of *gata* meaning 'street' which can be found in and around the Lace Market. Within a relatively short distance of each other are Fletcher Gate, the street of 'fleshers' or butchers, Pilcher Gate for the makers of 'pilches' or furs, Warser Gate, Barker Gate and Fisher Gate. Danish control of Nottingham continued until about 920 when Edward the Elder arrived in the borough, having returned most of the Midlands to Saxon rule. With defensive considerations in mind, the borough's fortifications were strengthened and a bridge was built over the Trent. This was probably the first ever bridge to span the Trent and its completion put Nottingham on a direct route between London and York, a position of strategic and commercial importance for the borough's future development.

Nottingham's natural and man-made advantages were soon to be recognised by another generation of settlers, this time from France. One of the first actions of the Normans was to establish a castle, though not inside the existing borough but at some distance to the west, set on a sandstone crag with a precipitous south-facing cliff. Originally the castle would have been constructed of timber but eventually a more solid castle was built from stone, with an inner and outer bailey, curtain walls, gatehouse and a moat. As time went on new streets and houses accumulated on the slope that led down from the castle towards the old borough. However, the life of this new community revolved around the new castle and Norman customs, so that quite rapidly Nottingham became a town of two boroughs, a 'French Borough' and an 'English Borough'. Each borough had its own law courts and borough officials, a situation that continued for centuries. And even after they were officially united, each borough continued to elect its own sheriff, until Corporation reforms in 1835. At an early stage in the French borough's development two parish churches were established, that of St Peter and St Nicholas, with St Mary's continuing to serve the English 'borough'.

Medieval Nottingham

From Domesday Book we know that there were at least 227 houses in Nottingham, and it is reasonable to estimate that the combined population of the two boroughs was between one and two thousand. Commerce was well advanced by the 11th century and the 120 burgesses mentioned in Domesday increased steadily in successive centuries; indeed their impact on commerce and local administration was to influence much of Nottingham's development up until the middle of the 19th century. It was the burgesses who controlled trade, took on apprentices, voted in elections and who held 'common' rights in the town's surrounding arable fields, pasture and meadow land. Important toll rights were granted to Nottingham in c.1155 when the town received its first royal charter from Henry II. The charter also permitted a market to be held on Fridays and Saturdays and local weavers were granted a monopoly of the production of dyed cloth. Possibly because the weekday market occupied an increasingly cramped site, on the edge of the English borough, a new Great Market was developed on a large, open space that lay midway between the English and French boroughs. On this same land, now known as Old Market Square or Slab Square, an eight-day trading fair was also established, the original version of what was later to become Goose Fair. This was once primarily a trading fair but is now famous for its fairground thrills and spills. To protect the newly enlarged town a stone wall was constructed, its principal course following what was to become Parliament Street, until it joined the Saxon borough's defences at its eastern end. It seems likely that most of the wall was built between 1267 and 1334, as a succession of 'murage' grants to finance building were made during those years. Few of the town's ancient gates or entrances survived much beyond the medieval period, with the exception of Chapel Bar, a once imposing structure with dual towers, but which by the time of its demolition in 1743 had fallen into a sadly dilapidated state. Beyond the walls there were institutions for the sick and needy. St Leonard's leper hospital stood north of the wall, while a second leper hospital is thought to have stood somewhere near Chapel Bar. Not far from Hollowstone, at the north end of the River Leen Bridge, John de Plumptre founded his Plumptre Hospital, an almshouse for 13 elderly widows 'bent by old age and depressed by poverty'. In the early 12th century a large Cluniac Priory was built at Lenton, about a mile west of Nottingham. Lenton Priory dominated the medieval town's spiritual life; its estates ran into several counties and its annual fair attracted people and trade from all over the Midlands.

Under a 1284 charter from Edward I the office of mayor was created, along with powers to regulate market trading and to arbitrate on issues of law. His office was supported by a coroner and two bailiffs, these officials forming the nucleus of a developing town council. In 1449 an important charter from Henry IV separated the town from the shire, granting it county status in its own right, while the two bailiffs were given the rather grander title of sheriff, one for each borough. At around the same time a major rebuilding of St Mary's church was begun which took more than twenty years to complete. A new west front was added, south aisle, clerestory, transept and central tower, complete with battlements and eight pinnacles. Incorporating the grandest elements of Perpendicular style, the builders created a town church that fully reflected the prosperity and confidence of the age.

From the middle of the 15th century the town council, or Corporation, became virtually a 'close' Corporation, dominated by a small number of wealthy families. Among those influential families were the Thurlands, whose ranks included Thomas Thurland, a wealthy wool merchant who was nine times mayor of Nottingham between 1442 and 1464. Thomas Thurland founded the gild of Holy Trinity in St Mary's church, which provided two chaplains to celebrate mass, and after his death he was buried in the church, where part of his tomb can still be seen.

Nottingham's towering castle, its town walls and handsome churches must all have been impressive features in the urban landscape. In contrast, however, its streets would have been for the most part unpaved and frequently muddy. Exceptions to this were Low, Middle and High Pavement which probably had a surface of cobbles. Most houses would have been timber-framed, of varying standards of workmanship, with less fortunate inhabitants occupying earthen or mud hovels or even cave houses cut out of sandstone. The streets were regularly walked by the Mickletorn Jury who reported 'nuisances', obstructions to the highways and encroachments on common land. Tanning and dyeing, both flourishing local industries, were a constant problem for the jury as their waste water spilled out over streets and polluted local water supplies.

As in any medieval town, crime of one sort and another was ever present. Itinerant justices held court sittings at regular intervals and from 1449 the town had its own quarter sessions. A charter of 1330 confirmed Nottingham's right to have its own gaol, so it is likely that a gaol was in existence even before that time. The county had its own gaol in the King's Hall (Shire Hall) on High Pavement.

Outside the town, Sherwood Forest provided refuge for outlaws, though none as famous as the renowned Robin Hood. Much of the evidence for Robin Hood's life and adventures comes in the form of rhymes, songs and ballads, handed down through the generations. A revised version of Piers Plowman (1377) refers to the 'rymes of Robyn Hood' and by the end of the Middle Ages, Robin Hood had become a favourite character in popular ballads and mummers' plays. Contemporary historical evidence for Robin Hood's existence is difficult to interpret, and countless books and articles have been written on the subject. But perhaps the air of mystery surrounding Robin Hood has itself become part of his enduring popularity.

From Civil War to Georgian Elegance

In Tudor times Nottingham settled into a period of relative peace and prosperity. It is true that by modern standards its sanitary provisions were rudimentary but the wealthier inhabitants were increasingly concerned with comfort and outward appearances. Following a visit to the town in 1540, John Leland, Henry VIII's antiquary, was sufficiently impressed to record that it was 'without exception in all England'. By Leland's time Nottingham's medieval fortifications had become largely redundant, and Leland himself noted that 'much of the waul is now down, and the gates, saving 2 or 3'. Yet Nottingham Castle, despite its poor state of repair, was to find itself in the thick of fierce fighting between Royalists and Parliamentarians during the Civil War. On 22 August 1642 Charles I raised his royal standard just outside the Castle (Standard Hill), hoping to rally supporters to the Royalist cause. In fact he found that Nottingham was a town of divided loyalties, and, as there seemed little hope of establishing Nottingham as a major

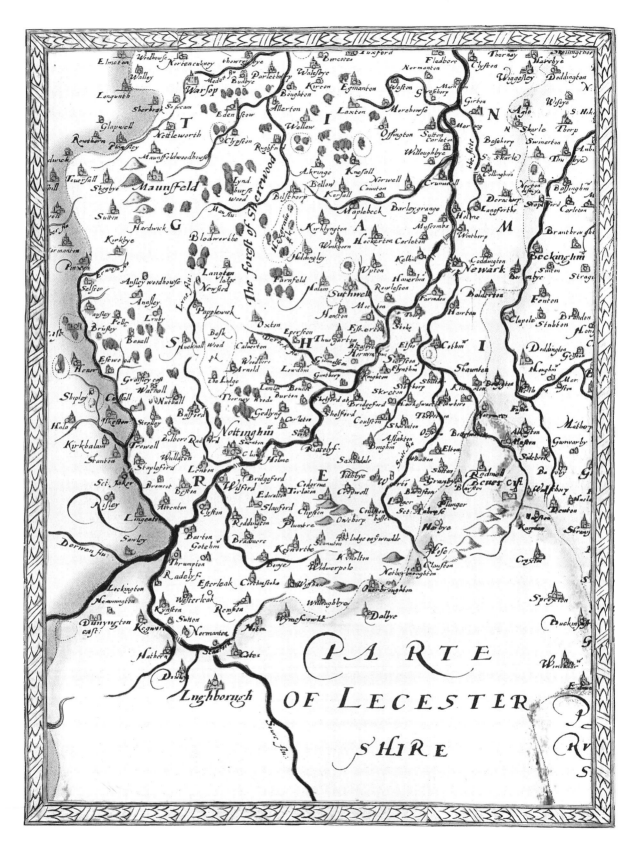

Part of Nottinghamshire from Saxton's map of 1576.

Royalist centre, he soon afterwards led his troops on to Shrewsbury. Taking advantage of this situation, Parliamentary troops garrisoned the Castle, turning it into a military stronghold for the remainder of the war. In September 1643 a force of about 600 Royalist troops from Newark managed to fight their way up to the Castle, some of them climbing onto the top of the tower of St Nicholas' church from where they fired down into the Castle yard. With the aid of reinforcements, the attack was eventually beaten off and, to prevent further use of St Nicholas' tower, the Castle governor, Colonel John Hutchinson, had the entire church demolished. Other attacks on Colonel Hutchinson and his soldiers were to follow but the Castle, if not always the town, remained under Parliamentary control throughout the war. And with the end of the war came the end of the old Castle. Fearing that it might be used yet again for military purposes, by one side or another, Colonel Hutchinson ordered that the Castle be pulled down.

When, in 1674, the first Duke of Newcastle decided to begin building a large new mansion on the site of the ruined Castle, it heralded a welcome period of growth and rebuilding for the whole town. The ducal residence sat fair and square on its crag of sandstone, having fine views over hill, dale and meadow for miles around. Leading town families soon followed the Duke's example, many choosing to build brick houses or to cover existing timber and plaster with brick courses. Some houses were laid out with gardens, and between many properties there were orchards and paddocks. The face of Nottingham was changing. On a visit in 1697 Celia Fiennes, who kept a remarkable account of her travels throughout England, described Nottingham as the 'neatest' town she had ever seen – she also noted the quality of Nottingham ale! In 1724 Daniel Defoe was equally impressed, remarking that it was 'one of the most pleasant towns in England'. Fashionable new houses appeared, usually built in brick, with elegant doorways, pediments and other period features. On Castle Gate there is a graceful row of houses, Nos. 43-47, which now serves as the City's Costume and Textile Museum. Further along, to the east, is Newdigate House, in which Marshal Tallard spent a genteel confinement after his capture at the battle of Blenheim, and where he kept a much-admired garden in the French style. On Low Pavement, Rothwell Willoughby built the tall and elegant Willoughby House, and, on High Pavement, William Hallowes chose to build a period house (County House) to take full advantage of views over the Trent meadows and hills beyond. Writing in 1815 the Nottingham historian, Blackner, commented that 'it forms an enchanting seat in the heart of the town'. Nor were public buildings neglected. A new Exchange was built to accommodate public meetings and the adjoining Shambles, with their butchers' shops and stalls, were given an overhaul. In 1744 it was also decided to rebuild the Guildhall on Weekday Cross, where the council conducted its day-to-day business. In 1770 a handsome new Shire Hall replaced the old dilapidated buildings on High Pavement, providing a more dignified setting for the business of quarter sessions. Nonconformist meeting houses also appeared in the town, with the Congregationalists establishing themselves on Castle Gate and the Presbyterians, later the Unitarians, on High Pavement. Located on these fashionable streets, both meeting houses attracted influential local families. By the end of the century High Pavement chapel had become a notable centre of political and intellectual life, and had founded its own charity school.

For aristocrats, the gentry and a growing merchant and professional class there was a full social round. There were musical parties, concerts, illuminations, dances, balls, theatrical entertainments, and every July horse races on the Forest drew crowds from all over England. Regular gatherings for cards, music, dancing, or simply the exchange of gossip, were held at the Assembly Rooms and Thurland Hall, while those who preferred outdoor pursuits might stroll along the banks of the Trent, go boating at Radford Grove, or wander to St Ann's well, to take the waters or try their hand at bowling. But not everyone was fortunate enough to indulge in these pleasures. For those without work or on low wages life was full of hardships and deprivations, and grievances frequently erupted in the form of riots. These usually centred on the Market Place, often being sparked off by shortages of food. Overcrowded housing was also becoming a problem in some parts of the town. In 1740 Nottingham's population was 9,890, but by 1801 it had risen to nearly 29,000. For the working classes in particular housing conditions became worse and worse, and with food shortages and political unrest ever present, the age of elegance was already under threat.

Hose, Lace and Luddism

By the end of the 18th century, Nottingham had become a leading centre for the manufacture of hosiery. Hose was produced on a frame, an ingenious device said to have been invented in 1589 by a Reverend William Lee of Calverton, a small Nottinghamshire village. Composed of more than 2,000 separate pieces, the frame was a remarkable technical achievement; a complicated system of springs, bars, levers and needles worked by a single operator through a combination of foot and hand movements. The operators, known as stockingers or framework knitters, sometimes established themselves in small workshops, but more usually they installed one or more frames in their own houses. Women and children were engaged in large numbers, winding yarn onto bobbins and seaming the flat pieces of material into finished hose. Framework knitting also grew to importance in the developing suburbs, places like Basford, Hyson Green and Radford; and in villages such as Arnold, Burton Joyce, Calverton, Lambley and Woodborough, transforming them into semi-industrial communities. Many framework knitters used cotton to produce hose, and, until Lancashire's cotton mills came to dominate cotton production, local supplies were in demand. James Hargreaves, who invented the spinning jenny, set up a cotton mill in Nottingham in around 1768, and Richard Arkwright is known to have built a mill somewhere between Hockley and Woolpack Lane, using horse power to drive the mill's machinery. Like hosiery, the production of lace was at first organised on a domestic basis. In 1809 John Heathcoat patented a highly successful process for the manufacture of lace on bobbin-net machines. A new breed of skilled operative was needed to work these machines. Lace operatives could earn substantially higher wages than stockingers and they generally lived in better built and more comfortable houses. An increasing number preferred to live a little beyond Nottingham, in Carrington, Hyson Green, New Basford, New Lenton and New Radford, where they could escape the overcrowding of inner Nottingham. The 'new' industrial communities attracted an artisan class which combined hard work and co-operative effort with strong nonconformist beliefs.

But for framework knitters a very different story was unfolding. Between 1809 and 1811 a succession of bad harvests began to push food prices up, while a drop in demand for hosiery caused wages to fall. To make matters worse some master hosiers exploited their control of the hosiery trade, cutting wages still further, breaking up traditional patterns of apprenticeship and charging excessive frame rents. During 1811 and 1812 growing unrest erupted into outbreaks of frame breaking, with attacks directed at the homes and frameshops of the more unscrupulous hosiers. Luddite attacks were frequently in the name of General Ludd, who supposedly lived in Sherwood Forest, though a Lady Ludd was also at the head of at least one gathering in the Market Square. Despite the introduction of special 'watch and ward' arrangements, the vigilance of local troops and sentences of transportation to Australia, the violence continued. Even after Parliament passed a Bill authorising the death penalty for framebreaking, a measure rigorously opposed by Lord Byron in his maiden speech in the House of Lords, there were further Luddite outbreaks. Failing to win major reforms, the framework knitters found themselves in an unenviable position, having virtually no political power and reduced to living in conditions of deprivation and poverty. And though Luddism had died out by 1817, Nottingham found itself at the centre of more riots in 1831. This time it was Chartist supporters who took to the streets, many of them framework knitters, in support of a campaign to extend the right to vote. On hearing that the Reform Bill had been rejected by the House of Lords, an angry mob gathered in Nottingham on 8 October 1831, their numbers swelled by Goose Fair visitors. The mob set off through the streets, attacking shops and houses. On arriving at Nottingham Castle, owned by the Duke of Newcastle (a leading opponent of the bill), the mob broke down the gates and set fire to the whole Castle, reducing it to a blackened shell. An attempt was also made to burn down Colwick Hall, the home of John Musters, another opponent of reform.

Nottingham in the 1840s was a much troubled town. It had its rich bankers, hosiers and merchants but it also had an increasingly vocal number of poor and disaffected residents. An 1844 report to the Health of Towns Commission stated 'that nowhere else shall we find so large a mass of inhabitants crowded into courts, alleys and lanes, as in Nottingham'. Worst of all were 8,000 back-to-back houses, built from the cheapest materials and in the form of enclosed courts that had little light or fresh air. For the rest of the century Nottingham Corporation fought to balance the need for change and industrial progress with the need to improve housing and public health.

A City in the Making

Nottingham's urgent need for public health and housing improvements was highlighted by a severe cholera epidemic in 1832. Nottingham was even running out of space to bury the dead, its overcrowded parish graveyards giving rise to unwholesome 'pestilential vapours'. Growing concern led to the opening of the General Cemetery in 1837, set in spacious grounds and planted with ornamental trees and shrubs. A few years later the Church (or Rock) Cemetery was established on a corner of the Forest, at the junction of Forest Road and Mansfield Road. Disease and infection claimed many victims, spreading rapidly through the town's untreated and rudimentary water supplies. Recognising the need for improvements a young water engineer, Thomas Hawksley, began a programme of work in the 1830s that gained him a national reputation. Hawksley designed new waterworks near Trent Bridge, driving filtered river water at high pressure through a network of pipes around the town. But despite this kind of pioneering work, Nottingham was still held back by its ancient boundaries. The town's expansion into the surrounding fields, meadows and 'waste' was fiercely resisted by the burgesses who held extensive 'common' rights, especially for grazing their cattle and sheep. Development had crept out along Mansfield and Derby Road, but most new housing could only be achieved by in-filling within the medieval boundaries. Then, in 1835, the Municipal Corporations Act finally broke the power of the old oligarchic Corporation, replacing it with a more democratic council and extending the vote to all ratepayers. The new Council lost little

Lace
for
Furnishing

CAREY & SONS, LTD.,

Salerooms :-- 45, Broad Street, NOTTINGHAM   21a, Old Change, LONDON
FACTORY   SOUTHWELL, Notts

time in securing the common lands for building and development by the promotion of parliamentary enclosure Acts. Two Acts of Parliament in 1839 began the enclosure process and a General Enclosure Act of 1845 enclosed the town's three large common fields: the Meadows, Clay Field and Sand Field.

Following enclosure, a tide of building spread rapidly across the former fields. New houses, factories and warehouses covered plot after plot, acre after acre, and with them came shops, churches, chapels and schools. To control the progress of enclosure and introduce much needed reforms for the whole town, the reformed Corporation established a series of committees with a wide range of responsibilities. However, the pace of development was rapid and both landowners and builders wanted to make profits from putting up houses of variable quality. Some parts of the newly expanded town, such as the Meadows and St Anns, were built in grid-iron patterns of red-brick terraces, while other areas, including the Park Estate and Alexandra Park, were developed with elegant villa residences for the middle and upper classes. In compensation for the loss of so much open space around the town, the Enclosure Act set aside 70 acres of land on the Forest for public recreation and part of the Sand Field was to be used for an Arboretum. Both parks were to prove invaluable assets to the town.

Nottingham's growth was aided by an ever expanding transport system. Bulky goods relied heavily on the waterways, and the opening of the Nottingham Canal in 1796 had provided an important link with Derbyshire via the Cromford Canal. The Beeston Canal, which joined with the Nottingham Canal at Lenton Chain and which was completed in the same year, linked with the River Trent, while a 30-mile long canal took a winding route between Nottingham and Grantham. The River Trent too was increasingly developed for commercial traffic, its difficult course between Nottingham and Newark eventually being tamed by a series of major locks. The railway era in Nottingham began in 1839 with the opening of the Midland Counties line between Nottingham and Derby, and other lines soon followed. Everywhere there were railway navvies at work, building cuttings, embankments, viaducts, bridges, tunnels and stations, both in and around Nottingham. On the roads it was all hustle and bustle as carriages, coaches, carts and wagons jostled to and fro, carrying passengers and goods of every kind. Regular passenger services began with privately-run horse bus and tram companies, replaced later with electric trams. Nottingham continued to expand rapidly, and in 1877 a Borough Extension Act took in Basford, Bulwell, Lenton, Radford, Carrington, Sherwood, Sneinton and part of Wilford. The new boundary increased Nottingham's area from 1,996 acres to 10,935 acres, and its population from 86,620 to 157,000. In 1897, the year of Queen Victoria's Diamond Jubilee, the town was elevated to city status. Industry was booming, especially the production of lace, which was sold all over the world. Machine-made lace had been pioneered by men like John Heathcoat and John Levers, inventors who combined practical skills with business acumen, and who could foresee the possibilities of the factory system. Attracted to Nottingham by a labour force already familiar with textiles, one lace firm after another built large lace factories at the edge of the town or in the suburbs, and most leading firms built prestigious head offices and warehouses in the maze of streets around St Mary's church, an area that eventually became known as the Lace Market. The imposing Thomas Adams & Page building on Stoney Street housed at least 500 employees and hundreds more were engaged as 'outworkers'.

Some of Nottingham's major industries were established in the late 19th century by entrepreneurs whose products became household names. The Raleigh Cycle Company was founded by Frank Bowden, who had taken up cycling to improve his health. Bowden bought an existing cycle workshop on Raleigh Street, but soon expanded into a former lace factory on Russell Street, producing 60 cycles a week. In 1896 Raleigh moved to yet bigger premises on Faraday Road, Lenton, expanding production from about 10,000 cycles in 1900 to 60,000 in 1913. When Jesse Boot left school at the age of 13, to help his mother run the family's herbalist shop on Goose Gate, it was to prove the beginning of one of the country's largest commercial empires. By his early 30s, Jesse Boot had established a growing network of shops, all supplied by his own factories and warehouses in and around Nottingham. John Player, who came to Nottingham from Saffron Walden, established his giant tobacco company in 1877, purchasing a small tobacco factory in Broad Marsh. Unlike his rivals, who sold their cigarettes and tobacco loose, Player put his products in distinctive packets and marketed them nationwide. By the turn of the century the company was employing over one thousand workers and new premises were opened in Radford.

Nottingham's growing population lived busy, hard working lives, but there was also a need for shops, schools, hospitals and recreation facilities. With its stalls and street sellers, the Market Place continued to act as a focus of commercial and social life, but in addition new department stores were opened to cater for fashionable society. On Long Row there was Griffin & Spalding and on King Street there was Jessop's, a distinctive store designed by local architect, Watson Fothergill. Sport of all kinds was popular. There were clubs for rowing, swimming, bicycling, cricket and football. Founded in 1862, Notts County (the 'Magpies') is the oldest League club in England and Nottingham Forest began just a few years later. As today, cricket has always been enthusiastically supported and in the 1880s the County Cricket Club won a series of victories in the county championships which gained the club a national reputation. On the Trent there was boating of all kinds, and a string of rowing clubs was established near Trent Bridge. For the musically inclined there were orchestral concerts, organ recitals, choral festivals, band concerts and glee club performances. Entertainment ranging from vaudeville to serious drama was on offer at local theatres, while a lively mix of drinking and robust pastimes of one kind and another was available at numerous public houses and taverns. And for everyone, young or old, rich or poor, there was the annual Goose Fair, held on the Market Place until 1927, after which it moved to the Forest. Other interests were met by the Mechanics' Institute, which had a large lecture hall, library and even a small museum. In 1874 agreement was reached between the Duke of Newcastle's trustees and the Corporation for the Castle to be converted into a museum and art gallery. The wounds of the Castle's stormy past were finally to be healed and a new future lay ahead. For those who enjoyed reading there were several subscription libraries, including the Bromley House Library on Angel Row. There had been a small public library on Thurland Street, but, in planning the University College buildings in the 1870s, the Corporation took the opportunity to incorporate a spacious new public library. University College became a focus of both learning and civic pride and its rapid expansion, coupled with financial help from Jesse Boot, led to the opening of an entirely new University campus at Highfields in 1928, and eventual independent university status. Many other public and private institutions, including schools and hospitals, also played their part in creating 20th-century Nottingham. It was a time of growth and change. Civic pride in the new Nottingham was expressed in the opening of the new Council House in 1929, built to replace the old Exchange. There were difficult years ahead, but Nottingham was set to face the future with hope, confidence and determination.

The Plates

Introduction

1. Charles I erects the Royal Standard in Nottingham, 1642.

2. A 1677 'Prospect of Nottingham' from Thoroton's *Antiquities of Nottingham*. There is no longer any trace of the town's medieval walls, but Chapel Bar, the ancient gateway into Nottingham from the west, remains a prominent feature. Chapel Bar was finally pulled down in 1743. On the right is St Peter's handsome spire and further behind is the tower of St Mary's church, set in the heart of the old English borough.

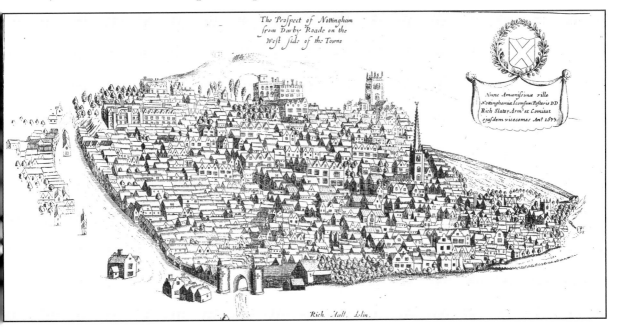

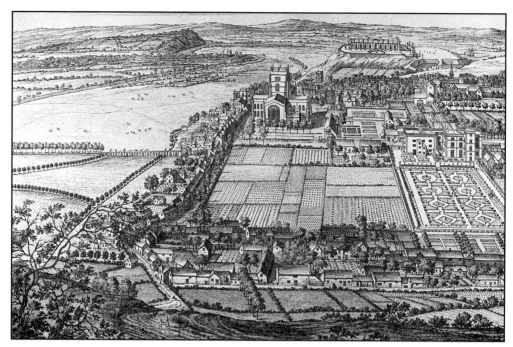

3. Jan Kip's 'East Prospect of Nottingham', 1707-8, shows an elegant 'garden town', with the Duke of Newcastle's recently completed Castle residence standing proudly on its crag of sandstone. Other major buildings include St Mary's church, which dominates the surrounding streets and houses, and the formal gardens of Pierrepont House. An arched causeway takes travellers over the meadows and River Leen while the River Trent takes a winding course past Wilford and Clifton Grove.

4. Badder and Peat's map of Nottingham in 1744 shows a town of fashionable houses, gardens, orchards and open spaces. Only a densely built-up area of streets and alleys between Long Row and Back Side (Parliament Street) hints at Nottingham's future housing problems.

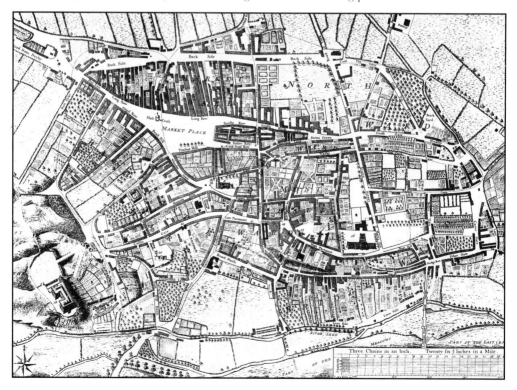

5. This view of Nottingham from the south, in 1846, depicts an almost idyllic pastoral scene. But in reality Nottingham had already become an industrial town; factory chimneys have appeared on the skyline and beneath Castle Rock a train makes its way towards the Midland Station.

6. An aerial photograph of the Lace Market, taken in 1927. Tall lace warehouses and other commercial buildings line the canyon-like streets of this distinctive area. In the foreground is High Pavement Chapel and, to its left, is Weekday Cross. At this point the Great Central railway emerges from a long tunnel from the Victoria Station, on its north to south route through Nottingham.

The Market Place

7. Nottingham Market Place in 1813, by the drawing master, Richard Bonington. Long colonnades of shops look out on to a tranquil scene, as fashionable society goes about its daily business. Yet at the same time the Market Place was frequently a focus for violent political gatherings and riots. The Exchange, on the east side of the Market Place, was built in the 1720s and served both as a town hall and to house the Shambles, a series of shops and stalls.

8. The Pot Market is in progress at the west end of the Market Place, c.1895. Behind the pot sellers, Market Street connects the Market Place with Parliament Street. Market Street was completed in 1865, replacing the narrow and dangerous Sheep Lane as part of an improvement scheme north of the Market Place.

9. Street sellers and hawkers ply their trade in the Market Place, *c*.1895. On market day you could buy anything from corn, poultry or cheese, to any number of home-made goods and knick-knacks. The air would have resounded with a multitude of street cries, gabble and laughter.

10. Queen Victoria's statue casts a regal eye over the Market Place and Exchange, *c*.1910. The statue was unveiled on 28 July 1905 by the Duke and Duchess of Portland. It was moved to the Victoria Embankment in 1953.

11.   End of an era – the last Goose Fair to be held in the Great Market Place, October 1927. Nottingham's Old Exchange has been demolished and in its place rises the new Council House, its future dome resembling a rocket ready for take-off. The market was transferred to King Edward Street.

12. Official opening of the new Council House by the Prince of Wales on 22 May 1929. The Prince and other dignitaries proceed along the Processional Way, watched by a huge crowd. The Council House included the council chambers, reception rooms and Mayor's apartments, while at the east end there were shops at ground level and offices above. The Council House was designed by T. Cecil Howitt and was built of Portland stone. Also in 1929 the Great Market Place was renamed the Old Market Square, though it has become popularly known as Slab Square.

Street Scenes

13. High Street, *c.*1890, a short but busy thoroughfare behind the Exchange buildings. On the right is Armitage Brothers, a firm of grocers founded by Samuel Fox Armitage, a prominent local Quaker. Further up the street is the piano, organ and music depot of Henry Farmer, and on the corner of High Street and Pelham Street is a piazza that was later removed for the building of a Boot's the Chemist store.

14. Lister Gate and the Walter Fountain, 1885. In the background is St Peter's church. The fountain was presented 'to the people of Nottingham' in 1866 by the son of John Walter who had represented Nottingham in Parliament. It cost £1,000 and was designed by local architect, Richard Sutton.

15. Wheeler Gate looking northwards from St Peter's Square, c.1895 – the strange appearance of the road surface may have been caused by street cleaning. As road traffic south increased, Wheeler Gate proved far too narrow and major widenings were undertaken in both 1885 and 1892.

16.   Parliament Street, looking towards Theatre Square, *c*.1900. A horse-drawn tram pulls a full load of passengers towards the Square, while laden carts take the same route over the cobbled road.

17.   Shoppers, browsers and stallholders mingle at the bottom of Angel Row, *c*.1890. On market days a variety of stalls extended from the Market Place along Angel Row. The *Bell Inn* was well placed to provide refreshment for shoppers, or anyone simply wanting to pass 'the time of day'. Its façade is thought to have been reconstructed in the 1830s, though parts of the building suggest medieval origins.

8.   Angel Row, from the corner of Market Street, *c*.1930. Between the Morris Wallpaper Co. Ltd. and Pearson & Pearson, he perambulator manufacturer, is the former Georgian town house of Sir George Smith, the Nottingham banker. From 822 this elegant building became the home of Bromley House Subscription Library, which continues to flourish up to the resent day.

19.   A view northwards up Mansfield Road from the junction of Melbourne Street and Shakespeare Street. The Young Men's Christian Association is at the corner of the two streets. On the right of the photograph and standing just behind Mansfield Road is the tower of Nottingham Brewery – the tower had an elaborate 'cap', with a tall pole. Beer was stored in large rock cellars, from which it was raised into the brewery yard by means of a steam lift.

20. A line of cabs alongside the drinking fountain at the top of Derby Road, *c*.1870. The area has since become known as Canning Circus, marking the junction at the head of Derby Road (Toll House Hill), Wollaton Street and Talbot Street.

21. In medieval times Drury Hill may have led towards a postern gate in the ancient town wall. Its narrow, winding course remained a well-used route from Narrow Marsh into Nottingham until 1969-71 when it was demolished to make way for the Broad Marsh Centre. This photograph was taken in 1906 from the bottom of Drury Hill.

Shops & Shopping

22. Pearson's family-run shop on Angel Row sold a wide variety of household goods, furnishings and toys, and had a long tradition of service to its customers. It was founded by Tom Pearson and his brother in 1889. This is an 1898 advertisement for the firm. Pearson's closed down in 1988.

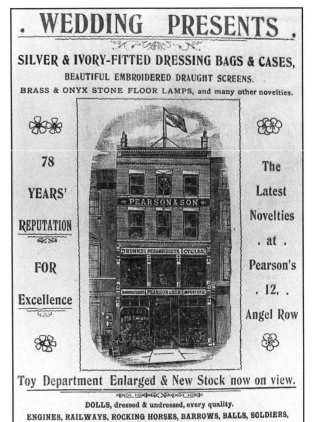

WEDDING PRESENTS

SILVER & IVORY-FITTED DRESSING BAGS & CASES,
BEAUTIFUL EMBROIDERED DRAUGHT SCREENS.
BRASS & ONYX STONE FLOOR LAMPS, and many other novelties.

78 YEARS' REPUTATION FOR Excellence

The Latest Novelties . at . Pearson's . 12, . Angel Row

Toy Department Enlarged & New Stock now on view.

DOLLS, dressed & undressed, every quality.
ENGINES, RAILWAYS, ROCKING HORSES, BARROWS, BALLS, SOLDIERS,
PRINTING PRESSES, WHIPS, MAGIC LANTERNS, etc.

PLEASE CALL AND LOOK ROUND. . . .

Pearson & Son, Ltd., 12, Angel Row

SISSON & PARKER

Booksellers & Stationers,

Wheeler Gate, NOTTINGHAM.

School Outfitters and Contractors, University Booksellers.

HIGH-CLASS LEATHER AND FANCY GOODS.

Home and Commercial Stationery, Fountain Pens and Stylos.

23. This advertisement for Sisson & Parker was used in commercial directories throughout the early 1900s. The site is now occupied by Dillon's.

24. Building plan by local architect Watson Fothergill for Jessop's new shop on King Street 1895. Fothergill's ornate decoration and accomplished style was much in demand for both private and public buildings in the Victorian and Edwardian periods. In 1866 Zebedee Jessop took over a small haberdashery and millinery store on Long Row. Business expanded rapidly and the move to new premises brought with it a reputation as one of Nottingham's leading department stores. Jessop's is now located in the Victoria Centre

25. Gunn & Moore, the famous sports shop, when it was at 49 Carrington Street, in the early 1930s. One of its specialities was cricket bats, as is evident from the shop frontage!

26.   A Nottingham Co-op delivery cart in 1905. In this photograph the well groomed horse and smartly attired man are posed carefully with their cart. Horse-drawn deliveries of provisions, especially bread, were common right up to the late 1930s.

27. Hucknall Road Co-operative shop, *c.*1930. The Co-operative movement grew out of a combination of temperance and nonconformity. The Nottingham Society had its origins in a meeting of the Lenton Temperance Society in 1863 which resolved to establish a Co-operative Society 'on the principle of opening a store for the sale of provisions, groceries, etc.'. Until 1906 the Society was known as the Lenton & Nottingham Co-operative Society Limited.

Nottingham Castle

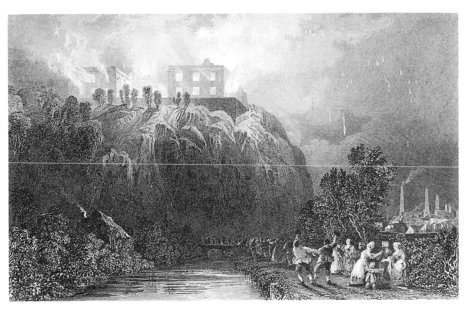

28. Nottingham Castle was burned down in 1831 by an angry mob of Chartist supporters. The mob took to the streets on hearing that Parliament had rejected the Reform Bill to extend the vote. A leading opponent of the Bill was the Duke of Newcastle, who owned Nottingham Castle.

29.   A garden party in the Castle grounds. After the Castle had been re-opened as a public Museum and Art Gallery in 1878, the grounds and gardens were popular for public celebrations, musical concerts and other entertainments. The North front, seen here, was restored in 1891.

30.   The Long Gallery of the Midland Counties Art Museum (Castle Museum) shortly after its opening by the Prince and Princess of Wales on 3 July 1878. Originally natural light through roof windows was the only source of illumination for the pictures. The new 'Art Museum' was greeted enthusiastically by Nottingham people who were able to view a mixture of local exhibits and items loaned by South Kensington Museum.

31.   Nottingham Castle's two 'wings' are clearly visible in this photograph of about 1880. In contrast to the Castle's stately repose, the scene below is very much from the workaday life of the town. Barges tied up at the Dukes Wharves until the construction of Castle Boulevard in 1884.

Hospitals

32. Nottingham General Hospital was founded in 1781 on land given by Nottingham Corporation. Benefactors to the new building included the Hon. Henry Cavendish of Chatsworth House, Sir Richard Arkwright and Peter Nightingale, the great uncle of Florence Nightingale. By the early 19th century there were severe shortages of space, especially on the 'fever' wards, and in 1854-6 the hospital was enlarged, by T.C. Hine, and a new chapel was also built.

33. A young patient on the Girls' Ward, c.1895. In 1869 a committee was formed to establish a hospital for sick children, and in that same year Russell House, which stood opposite the General Hospital, was opened with facilities for eight patients. New buildings were gradually added, but in 1900 a new children's hospital was opened in Forest House, Mapperley.

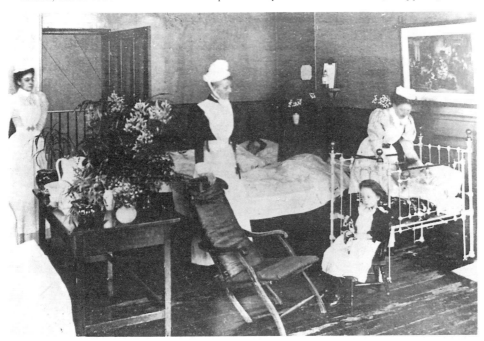

34.   The Midland Institution for the Blind was erected in 1853 on the corner of Clarendon Street and Chaucer Street. Instruction for the children was based on an enlightened regime that included musical tuition, craftwork and gymnastic exercises. There were opportunities for singing in a local church choir and a shop was opened for the sale of work produced by the children.

35.   The Coppice Hospital (Lunatic Asylum), Ransom Road, Mapperley, was designed by T.C. Hine and built between 1857-9. Funds were largely raised by voluntary subscriptions and originally only private patients were admitted.

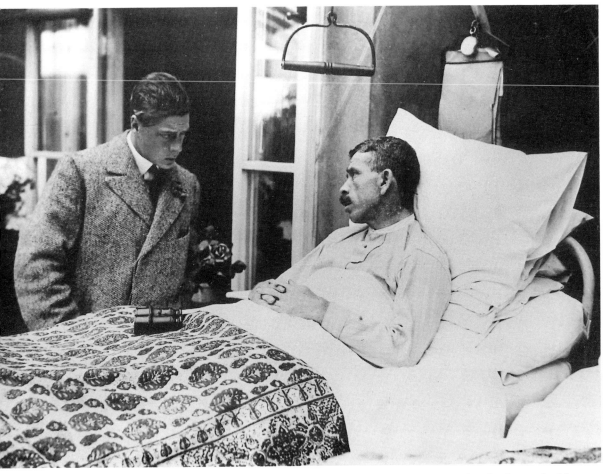

36.   The Prince of Wales visits patients at Ellerslie House, Gregory Boulevard, a Home for paralysed sailors and soldiers, on 1 August 1923. Great concern is evident in the Prince's face.

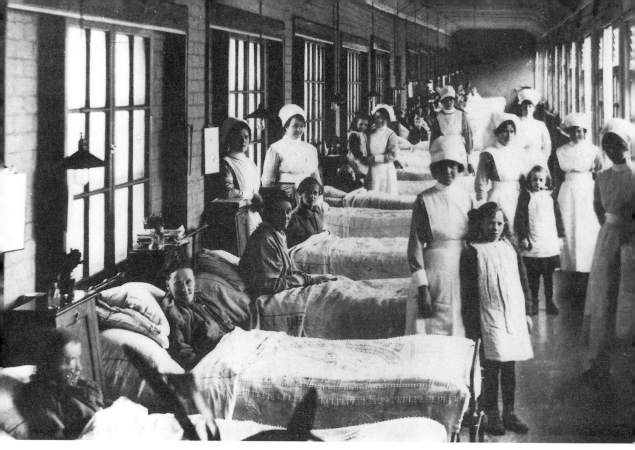

37. Bagthorpe Sanatorium ward in 1919, part of the Nottingham Union Workhouse which was built in 1903. Bagthorpe replaced an earlier Poor Law workhouse on York Street which was demolished for the construction of the Victoria Station. Bagthorpe eventually became part of the City Hospital.

38. Although only a short distance from the city centre, Collin's Almshouses on Friar Lane preserved an area that was a world away from the cares of everyday life. The almshouses were founded under the 1709 will of Abel Collin, a local mercer. Pevsner described them as 'A lovely group, one of the best almshouses of its date in England'. Sadly they were demolished in 1956.

WHEREAS,

Several **EVIL-MINDED PERSONS** have assembled together in a riotous Manner, and **DESTROYED** a **NUMBER** of

FRAMES,

In different Parts of the Country :

THIS IS

TO GIVE NOTICE,

That any Person who will give Information of any Person or Persons thus wickedly

BREAKING THE FRAMES,

Shall, upon CONVICTION, receive

50 GUINEAS

REWARD.

And any Person who was actively engaged in **RIOTING**, who will impeach his Accomplices, shall, upon **CONVICTION**, receive the same Reward, and every Effort made to procure his Pardon.

☞ Information to be given to Messrs. **COLDHAM** and **ENFIELD**.

Nottingham, March 26, 1811.

39. In 1811 and 1812 conditions of near starvation for some framework knitters, low wages, and high prices led to frequent disturbances and even riots. Frame breaking, some undertaken in the name of General or Ned Ludd, was concentrated on the homes and workshops of wealthy hosiers. The authorities introduced a variety of measures to try to control the situation, among them new 'watch and ward' arrangements and rewards for informants.

40.   An election riot takes over the Market Place in 1865. Many of those who assembled came from surrounding villages and towns, many coming by special trains. On arrival they were 'set upon by a violent rabble', though police and soldiers eventually quelled the riot. The meeting was to have been addressed by Messrs. Paget and Morley, but in the event they did not make an appearance. (From a painting by John Holland titled 'Fight for the Platform'.)

41. Shire Hall, High Pavement, decorated for the coronation of George V in 1911. Justice was administered here in a succession of buildings from medieval days. The central façade shown in this photograph was built in 1770 to a design by James Gandon, but there are Victorian additions, including the ornate pediment. Its courtrooms were built to impress but at the rear of the Hall was a forbidding array of cells, some fashioned out of rock, including one that was nothing more than a rock pit. Public hangings were originally conducted in front of Shire Hall but were transferred to a 'hanging yard' behind the building after 1877.

42. Illustration from a contemporary broadside on the hanging of William Clayton, aged 18 years, at Shire Hall on 2 April 1833. Clayton was executed for the 'wilful' murder of Samuel Kay, a butcher who had been returning home to Sutton-cum-Lound from Bawtry Market. He was found lying on a manure heap with a savage knife wound in his neck, his pockets 'rifled of their contents'.

43. A coach has arrived at the Judge's Lodgings (County House), High Pavement, on a summer's day in 1895. The Lodgings were originally a private house built by William Hallowes in the early 18th century. Then, in 1833, the house was sold to the county magistrates as a Judge's Lodgings, and was substantially enlarged. From 1949 it has been occupied by Nottinghamshire County Council's Archives Office, which houses archives from the 12th century onwards. Its collections include Nottingham's historic borough archives.

44. The Nisi Prius Court was remodelled following a fire in 1877 and reflects all the grandeur of the Victorian age. Nisi Prius was the name of writs that originated civil proceedings at the Westminster courts but which were held locally so that parties could more easily travel to the proceedings.

45. The House of Correction, St John's Street, *c.*1895. It was also known as St John's Prison as it was built on the site of the former convent of the St John's Hospitallers whose estates in Nottingham passed to the Corporation at the time of the Dissolution. Among the prison's deterrents was a treadmill, installed in 1825, which raised water from an underground reservoir. In 1891 the prisoners were transferred to a new gaol at Bagthorpe and the House of Correction was subsequently demolished as it lay in the path of the new King Edward Street.

46. Nottingham Town Hall and Prison, Weekday Cross, 1791. A prison had existed on the site, probably from early medieval times. In 1744 the building was substantially enlarged, with an extension to the upper floors, a new brick façade and a row of 10 wooden pillars. Its prison accommodation, however, was notoriously cramped and included a condemned cell and debtors' prison. The whole building was cleared for the construction of the Manchester, Sheffield and Lincolnshire railway line which ran near Weekday Cross.

THE SCHEDULE.

PORTRAIT AND DESCRIPTION OF HABITUAL DRUNKARD.

Name and alias Sarah Clay

Residence 15, Pomfret Street

SARAH CLAY.
Book 37. Folio 115.

Place of business or where employed None

Age 40

Height 4 ft. 11 ins.

Build Stout

Complexion Fresh

Hair Brown

Eyes Grey

Whiskers

Moustache

Shape of nose Flat

Shape of face Round

Peculiarities or marks Teeth missing from upper jaw

Profession or occupation Charwoman

Date and nature of conviction 6th February, 1903
Fined 10/- or 7 days

Court at which convicted Guildhall, Nottingham

N.B.—Should any known Habitual Drunkard attempt to purchase or obtain any intoxicating liquor at any premises licensed for the sale of intoxicating liquor by retail or at the premises of any registered Club it is requested that the licensed person or the person refusing to supply the liquor will, as soon as practicable, give information of such attempt to the City Police in order that the law may be enforced.

To the Licensee of the Generous Briton
To the Secretary of the Registered Club Island Street

Whose special attention is called to this Case.

47. Opened in 1888, the new Guildhall on the corner of Burton Street and South Sherwood Street replaced the Weekday Cross buildings. A spacious basement housed a network of prison cells and the police offices, while on the ground floor there were the court rooms, magistrates' offices and the Chief Constable's room. On the first floor a Grand Jury Room was used for the Assizes as well as Corporation committee meetings.

48. A portrait and description of Sarah Clay, a charwoman, convicted on 6 February 1903 as a 'Habitual Drunkard'. Under a Licensing Act of 1902 any person convicted as a drunkard was to be reported to the police by licensees for a period up to three years after the conviction date.

Church & Chapel

49. 'A Polite Congregation' at St Mary's, Nottingham's largest parish church, 1796. This illustration was etched by Isaac Cruikshank and drawn by G. Woodward for his *Eccentric Excursions* in which he satirises contemporary Nottingham society. He describes St Mary's as a 'handsome Gothic structure' but complains of the 'fashionable small-talk' during services and of the 'incessant bows and curtsies' as the congregation departs.

50. St Mary's church, *c.*1900, with a cab rank along High Pavement. A church had probably stood on the site since pre-Conquest times, and later served the old Saxon borough. In the 15th century it was rebuilt in a style that matched Nottingham's growing status and prosperity. In the Victorian period major restoration work was undertaken on the west front and clerestory windows. Near the west door there is an unusual gravestone of baked pipeclay, erected in 1714 by William Sefton, a Nottingham pipemaker, in memory of his two daughters.

51. St Peter's is an elegant church which has always been an island of tranquillity in the hustle and bustle of city centre life. The building on the right is the 'new' General Post Office, opened in 1848 but replaced in 1898 by the Queen Street Post Office.

52. Holy Trinity Church made what the architectural historian, Pevsner, described as 'a fine accent in the skyline of Nottingham', because of its needle-like spire. Holy Trinity was built in 1841 in response to the town's growing population but was demolished when the whole of Trinity Square was redeveloped for a new multi-storey car park and shopping area. This photograph dates from c.1895.

53. St Barnabas (Roman Catholic) Cathedral, Derby Road, was built between 1841 and 1844 by the famous architect, Augustus Welby Pugin. Funds for its construction came largely from the Earl of Shrewsbury. Among its notable features is the 'proud steeple' which stands 150 ft. high, and a series of Pugin's original stained glass (aisle) windows.

54. Wesleyan chapel, Halifax Place, *c.*1880. Founded in the full tide of Methodism in 1798, this chapel was rebuilt on the same site in 1847. For many years it remained a vital focus of religious and social life but, as the area around Halifax Place became overtaken by business premises and warehouses, its membership began to fall. It finally closed in 1930.

55. Derby Road Baptist chapel, *c.*1902. The chapel was founded by members of the Nottingham Spaniel Row Baptist congregation in 1847 and building on the Derby Road premises began in 1849. However, by the 1960s changes in local population patterns and other factors prompted moves towards union with the Lenton Baptists. In 1964 the two congregations combined and the Derby Road building was closed.

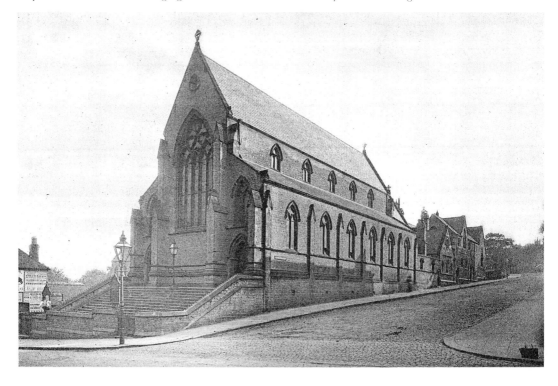

56. High Pavement Unitarian chapel dominates the cluster of buildings in Narrow Marsh in about 1930. Built in 1876 to replace an earlier chapel on the same site, it included a stained glass window designed by Burne Jones.

57. William Booth, founder of the Salvation Army, was born in Notintone Place, Sneinton, in 1829. After leaving school, William was apprenticed to a pawnbroker in Goosegate where he must have encountered the crushing poverty that his 'army' would later confront. He moved to London in 1849 and eventually joined a mission group in the East End where he developed his ideas for the formation of a Salvation Army. A small museum in the William Booth Memorial Complex at Notintone Place records Booth's life and work, and a statue of him stands in the centre of the Complex.

Cemeteries

58. The main entrance to Nottingham General Cemetery, and almshouses, 1838. Demands for a new cemetery grew after a cholera epidemic of 1832 and were heightened by a shortage of burial plots in the town graveyards. The General Cemetery was opened early in 1837, at first for Church of England burials, and from 1856 for 'dissenters' as well. The grounds were laid out with trees, shrubs and wide footpaths.

59. A view over the General Cemetery looking towards Nottingham High School on the skyline. The cemetery occupied a total of 18 acres of land that dipped down from Derby Road towards Waverley Street. It was originally run by a private company established under an 1836 Act of Parliament.

60. A turn-of-the-century photograph taken across the Church Cemetery looking towards St Andrew's church. This cemetery was opened in 1856 on land at the corner of Mansfield Road and Forest Road. Part of the cemetery included 'a remarkable series of caverns scooped out of the living rock', which still exists today. Among the notables buried in the Church Cemetery are the architect, Watson Fothergill, and the philanthropist, the Rt. Hon. A.J. Mundella.

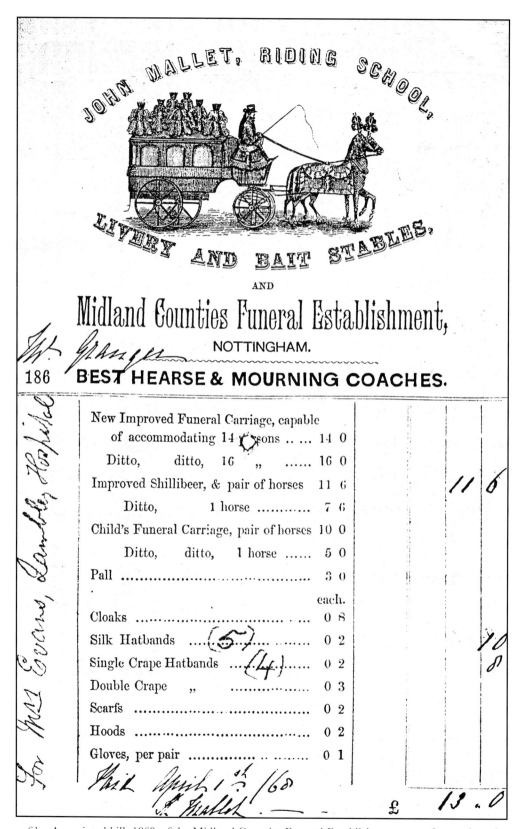

JOHN MALLET, RIDING SCHOOL,

LIVERY AND BAIT STABLES,

AND

Midland Counties Funeral Establishment,

NOTTINGHAM.

BEST HEARSE & MOURNING COACHES.

	£ s. d.	
New Improved Funeral Carriage, capable of accommodating 14 persons	14 0	
Ditto, ditto, 16 „	16 0	
Improved Shillibeer, & pair of horses	11 6	*11 6*
Ditto, 1 horse	7 6	
Child's Funeral Carriage, pair of horses	10 0	
Ditto, ditto, 1 horse	5 0	
Pall	3 0	
	each.	
Cloaks	0 8	
Silk Hatbands ...(5)...	0 2	*10*
Single Crape Hatbands ...(4)...	0 2	*8*
Double Crape „	0 3	
Scarfs	0 2	
Hoods	0 2	
Gloves, per pair	0 1	
	£	*13 . 0*

Paid April 1st /68
J. Mallet

61. A receipted bill, 1868, of the Midland Counties Funeral Establishment, one of a number of undertaking firms. Victorian funerals were highly elaborate, requiring ornate mourning attire in keeping with the solemn occasion. In this instance payments were made for a funeral carriage, horses, silk and crepe hatbands.

Industry

62. A hand frame knitter at work, *c*.1900. The hand, or stocking frame, is thought to have been invented by William Lee, a Nottinghamshire clergyman, as early as 1589. Composed of more than 2,000 parts, the frame required great dexterity and concentration, relying on a combination of hand and foot movements for its operation. In the 19th century there were thousands of framework knitters in Nottingham, some working in small workshops, others in converted attics or upper storeys of their own homes.

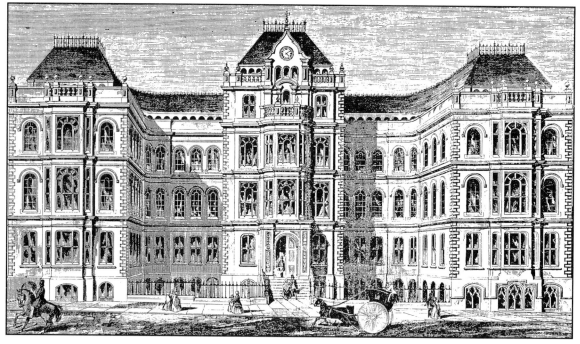

63. The lace premises of Messrs. Thomas Adams, Page and Company, on Stoney Street. The building, one of the finest in the Lace Market, was designed by T.C. Hine and included a library, classroom and chapel. It housed at least 500 workers on lace finishing and distribution, and hundreds more were employed as out-workers.

64. The main lace dressing room at Thomas Adams, 1914. In the early 1900s one-third of the city's working population was engaged in the manufacture of lace. In addition to the demand for fashion wear, there was a seemingly insatiable demand for lace curtains and firms like Thomas Adams were at the forefront of what had become a world-wide trade.

65. Lace clipping room at the premises of Birkin & Co. This photograph was taken in 1914 during a visit by George V and Queen Mary. Thomas Isaac Birkin, son of Richard Birkin the firm's founder, had extensive factories in New Basford and prestigious office and warehouse accommodation on Broadway, in the Lace Market. Birkin was also responsible for developing Forest Fields for housing.

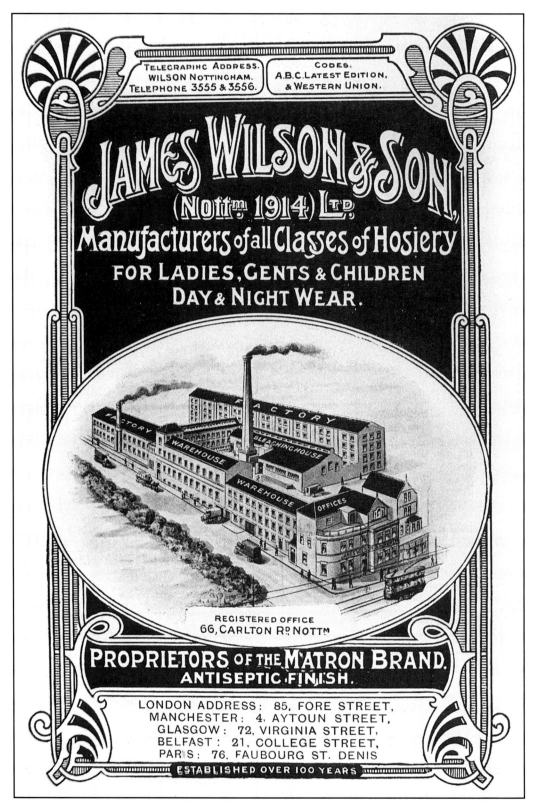

66.　A commercial directory advertisement for James Wilson & Son, hosiery manufacturers of Carlton Road, Nottingham. From its domestic beginnings in framework knitting, the manufacture of hosiery became a large-scale factory industry employing thousands of workers.

67. Shipstone's Star Brewery at New Basford, c.1920. Founded in 1852 by James Shipstone, the firm was carried on later by his two sons, James and Thomas. Local firms like Shipstone's inherited a brewing tradition that began in medieval days, with fine ales brewed in Nottingham's caves and rock cellars.

68. Shipstone's dray horses were a familiar sight on Nottingham's streets until well after the war. This advertisement appeared in a 1939 Nottingham *Handbook*.

69. Women at work in the cigarette packing department at Player's No. 2 Factory, Radford, *c*.1938. The company was founded by John Player, a former draper's assistant, who bought a small tobacco factory in Broad Marsh, in 1877. While his competitors sold their tobacco loose, John Player sold his tobacco and cigarettes in distinctive packets and devised popular brand names like 'Navy Cut'. Commercial success soon followed and by the 1880s the company was developing a huge new factory complex in Radford. John Player himself died in 1884 but his two sons, John Dane and William Goodacre Player, continued to expand the business. In response to foreign competition in the early 1900s John Player & Sons amalgamated with 12 other British companies to form Imperial Tobacco, though the Player's title and brand names were retained.

70. Carts and lorries at the loading docks of Player's No. 1 Factory, Beckenham Road, Radford, c.1928.

71. Raleigh Cycle Company assembly shop in 1922. Raleigh was founded by Frank Bowden, a wealthy lawyer, who had taken up cycling to help his recovery from a serious illness. In 1887 he bought a small cycle workshop on Raleigh Street, soon expanding into other premises on Russell Street. In 1896 Raleigh moved into even bigger premises on Faraday Road, Lenton, where production grew from 10,000 bicycles in 1900 to 60,000 by 1913.

1922
Raleigh Assembly Shop

72. From these modest premises on Goose Gate Jesse Boot ran a small herbalist's shop that was to become the Boot's Pure Drug Company, one of the largest retail empires in the country. To supply the growing network of shops, manufacturing premises were built in Nottingham and in 1930-2 a large industrial complex was built near Beeston. Jesse Boot became Lord Trent in 1929.

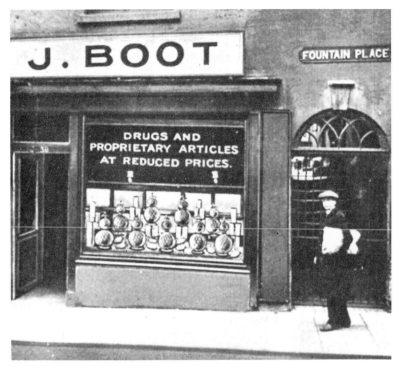

73. Coal picking in the screens at Clifton Colliery in about 1895. By the end of the century the colliery was employing around 1,000 men and boys, many from the Meadows area of Nottingham.

74. Vigorous spring cleaning at the Armitage family home, Blenheim House, St Ann's Hill, 1899. Domestic staff in large households were employed in an endless round of tasks. The Armitage family ran a flourishing grocery business in Nottingham.

Entertainment

75. A photo booth at Goose Fair in the 1890s. Nottingham is known to have had an autumn fair from at least the 13th century. How the fair acquired its unusual title is not certain but one theory is that it derives from the driving of thousands of geese for sale at the fair. In medieval times the fair was of primary importance for trade, but in more recent times the crowds have come for the sideshows, novelty attractions and daring rides.

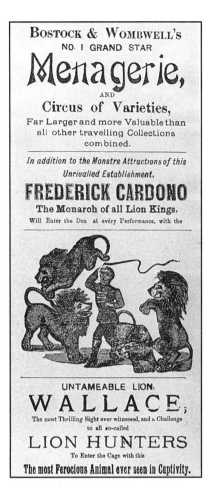

76. No visit to Goose Fair was complete without seeing Bostock & Wombwell's Menagerie, where audiences might gaze in wonder at a bizarre range of 'zoological specimens' or stare wide-eyed at confrontations between man and beast. By the 1880s the fair had been reduced to three days' duration. Mechanical rides and roundabouts began to dominate the sideshows and stalls, though Bostock & Wombwell's continued to attract the crowds.

77. The first cake-walk at Goose Fair drew large crowds in 1908. On the left is Queen Victoria's statue, later moved to the Victoria Embankment, and on the right is Griffin & Spalding, the fashionable department store.

78.   The big wheel has always been a popular ride at Goose Fair, combining excitement with a bird's-eye view of the whole fair. This photograph shows the big wheel in 1907.

79. Trips down the River Trent on a pleasure steamer were always popular. They started from a series of landing stages near Trent Bridge where it was also possible to hire rowing boats and other pleasure craft. In the background is the Midland Industrial Exhibition, opened in May 1903 but destroyed by fire only a year later.

80. A review of the Robin Hood Rifles on the Forest, one of a series of events which commemorated Queen Victoria's Diamond Jubilee in 1897. Beyond the Forest carriages are drawn up on open land which was later occupied by the Manning School. The Forest was set aside for public recreation by the 1845 Enclosure Act.

81. The Prince of Wales is escorted by the Mayor, Alderman E.L. Manning, and other civic dignitaries at a 'Review of Scholars' on the Forest in 1923.

82. Children and mothers enjoying a day in the fresh air at the Arboretum, *c.*1920. On its opening day, on 11 May 1852, 'a vast multitude' gathered both inside and outside the park, there was dancing and games, and bands played until half past eight in the evening. The bandstand was erected in 1907, following a petition to the Corporation signed by several hundred ratepayers.

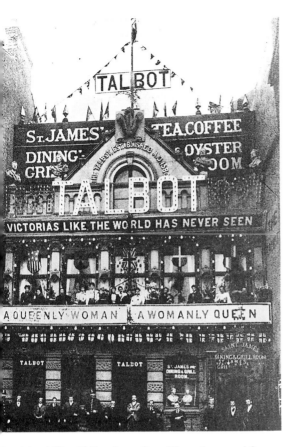

3. (*above*) The *Talbot*, Long Row West, decorated for Queen Victoria's Diamond Jubilee in 1897. In its heyday the *Talbot* was a showpiece of Victorian splendour. Its bars and balconies were encrusted with ornate statues and decorative china, it boasted a wide range of musical entertainments and its dining and grill room offered a full and varied menu.

4. (*above right*) Nestling under the Castle walls in about 1935 is the *Trip to Jerusalem*, reputed to be the oldest public house in England. According to legend, the Crusaders paused here for refreshment on their way to fight in the Holy Land. Underneath the pub, part of which is built into the sandstone, is a series of rock chambers.

5. (*right*) Once a busy though unexceptional coaching inn, the *Black Boy* on Long Row became a major centre of social life after it was rebuilt and enlarged by Watson Fothergill in 1887. Fothergill succeeded in retaining the colonnaded way of Long Row, while at the same time adding a characteristic frontage. Sadly it did not survive modern redevelopments.

86. These smartly dressed passengers – hats were evidently very much in fashion – were members of the Sports and Social Club of the Trent Motor Traction Company, assembled for a charabanc outing in 1926.

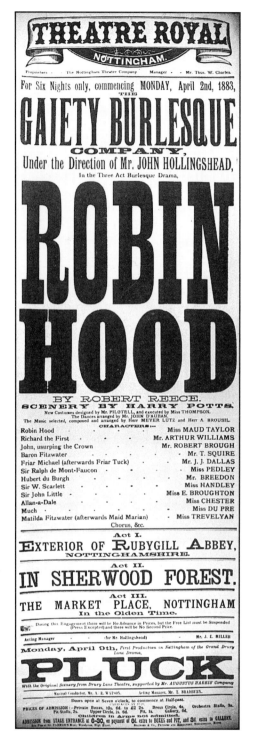

87. (*left*) The Theatre Royal opened on 25 September 1865, bringing the town much needed relief from a long summer of election riots. Reporting on the opening night, when Sheridan's 'School For Scandal' was performed, a local newspaper commented that the crowded house 'presented a scene of gaiety and splendour which we may safely assert was not to be met with that evening in any theatre in England'.

88. (*right*) The Empire Theatre stood on South Sherwood Street. In the 1920s its programmes reflected a desire after the First World War to break away from Victorian and Edwardian conventions, to experiment with new styles of dress, to travel and to take life a little less seriously.

89. A 1910 photograph showing both the Theatre Royal, on the left, and, facing South Sherwood Street, the Empire. The prolific theatre architect Frank Matcham had a hand in both these theatres, rebuilding the interior of the Theatre Royal in 1897 and designing the Empire at around the same time, under a contract with Moss Empires. The Empire opened in 1898, closed in 1958, and was finally demolished in 1969.

90. A new age of entertainment dawned in the 1930s with the opening of large new picture houses, like the Savoy Cinema on Derby Road. They catered for mass audiences and combined fashionable design with the latest technology.

91.   An early B.B.C. broadcasting control room in Nottingham, 1928. On the telephone is C.H.J. Wheeler, the engineer-in-charge. Another engineer sits at the control panel and an assistant keeps a watchful eye behind the switchboard.

Sport

92. A cricket match is played, *c.*1848, on grounds between the newly opened Midland Station on Station Street (left) and the Nottingham Canal (right).

93. Trent Bridge cricket ground in the 1890s – a proud groundsman surveys the greensward on a warm summer's day. Cricket in Nottingham can be traced back to the 1770s when a Nottingham 'Club' played several matches against Sheffield. Early matches were played on the Forest but in 1838 a new ground was established at Trent Bridge. A pavilion was built in 1872, though this was replaced at considerable cost by a new one in 1886 (as appears in the photograph). Additional seating and other facilities were built in 1898.

94.   This photograph of the England team was taken at Trent Bridge during the England versus Australia Test Match i June 1899. *Back Row*: Titchmarsh (Umpire); G.H. Hirst (Yorkshire); T. Hayward (Surrey); W. Gunn (Notts.); J.T. Hearne (Middlesex); W. Storer (Derbyshire); W. Brockwell (Reserve). *Middle Row*: C.B. Fry (Sussex); Prince Ranjitsinhji (Sussex); Dr. W.G. Grace (Capt.); F.S. Jackson (Yorkshire); Barlow (Umpire). *Front Row*: W. Rhodes (Yorkshire); J.T. Tyldesley (Lancashire).

5. A team photograph of Notts. County Football Club at the turn of the century. Notts. County can trace its origins back to a meeting in 1862, making it the oldest League club in existence. In its early days the team included several famous cricketers, including George Parr and Richard Daft. County played on Trent Bridge Cricket Ground until 1910 when they moved to Meadow Lane.

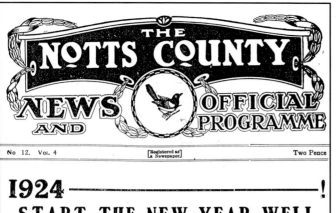

96. A 1924 front cover of Notts. County Football Club's official matchday programme. The club's nickname of 'The Magpies' is echoed in the magpie depicted in the programme's title heading.

97. A tense moment in a match between Nottingham Forest and Tottenham Hotspur on 4 September 1937. Nottingham Forest joined the Football League in 1892. Playing originally on the Forest racecourse, the club later moved to a ground in the Meadows and finally to the City ground which opened in 1898.

98. Nottingham Rowing Club was founded on 4 July 1862 at the *Union Inn*. The club began with a subscription of six pence a week, to go towards the purchase of racing boats so that members would be able 'to compete at neighbouring regattas and for encouraging rowing on the River Trent'. One of the club's social highlights was an annual dinner, usually accompanied by songs and humorous recitations.

99. 'Bendigo', the famous Nottingham prize fighter. Bendigo was born in 1811 in New Yard, Parliament Street, the last of 21 children. His real name was William Abednego Thompson. He started boxing at the age of 16 and soon established himself as a leading exponent of the 'art'. He continued to box until the age of 40, when he beat his last opponent after 49 rounds. In later life he became a vigorous preacher. He died in 1880, aged 69, and was buried in Bath Street cemetery.

100.   Members of the Castle Cycle Club pose for a club photograph outside the *Old Elm Tree* public house at Hoveringham in around 1885. The club arranged excursions and competitions. For some years its president was the Duke of Portland.

101. From Victorian times cycling was popular with women. It was both an enjoyable sport, and a convenient means of transport. This Raleigh Cycle Company poster of 1932 emphasised the speed, freedom and excitement of cycling. By this time, Raleigh and other cycle companies were producing a wide range of ladies bicycles, including roadsters and tourist models.

102. Swimming was an ever popular pastime, whether for sport, fun or health. This photograph shows the Exhibition Bath *c.*1914, part of the Victoria Baths, Gedling Street, Sneinton. Opened in 1896, these baths were built by the Corporation, replacing an earlier dilapidated building. In addition to the baths there were public wash-houses and laundry facilities.

103. Bowling on the Forest, 1914. This postcard was sent in the last carefree summer before the outbreak of the First World War. The bowling greens are still in use today.

Education

104. William Goodacre's Standard Hill Academy, 1848. A prospectus of the time proclaimed that the school combined 'the advantages of a town residence, with the pure air and retirement of the country'. Young gentlemen were instructed in 'sound grammatical Knowledge and a Pure Accent', reading, writing, mathematics, science, Latin and Greek, drawing 'by an eminent artist' and French 'by a native'.

105. On 18 October 1866 Lord Belper laid the foundation stone of the new Free Grammar (High) School, on a site between the Arboretum and the Forest. The new school replaced an earlier building on Stoney Street. On the east side of the central tower was the Classical (Upper) School, on the west side the English (Lower) School. A recreation area for the boys was hollowed out of the sandstone below the school buildings.

106. A chemistry lesson in one of the science labs at Mundella School, c.1906. Anthony Mundella began his working life as a framework knitter in Leicester, then in later years he moved to Nottingham where he entered into a successful business partnership with the hosier, Benjamin Hine. He became a prominent Liberal politician and was a well-liked public figure.

107. A group photograph of standard VI of Blue Bell Hill School, St Ann's, in the early 1900s. And not a smile to be seen! The school opened on 30 April 1883 and had separate departments for infants, junior and senior pupils. It was originally a Board School, run under the terms of the 1870 Education Act which allowed for the setting up of local School Boards to extend education to as many children as possible. Under Acts of 1876 and 1880, education was made compulsory for all children up to the age of ten.

108. Five-year-old pupils in the infants' section of the William Crane School, Aspley, involved in a 'shop' project, 1938. William Crane School was one of a new generation of inter-war schools, many of which were built at the centre of large new housing developments.

109. Children line up for an inspection by the school nurse, 1938. The Schools Medical Service began in 1907 with the appointment of two school nurses and two medical officers. By 1938 there were five medical officers, 16 school nurses, consultants, dental officers, a speech therapist, a psychologist, an ophthalmologist assistant and an 'electro therapeutist'.

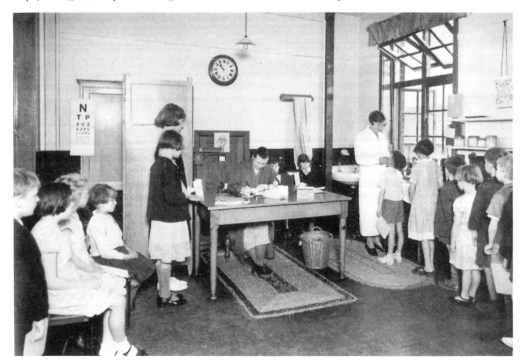

110.   Sculpture students at the College of Art, Waverley Street, 1939. Built in 1863-5, the College of Art rapidly gained a leading reputation for the range of its courses. As well as traditional art courses, students could study lace design, hosiery production, dress making and design, book binding and pottery. From the 1930s there were also classes in photography.

111.   Following a public meeting in 1837 a constitution was agreed for a Mechanics' Institute. In 1845 a new building was opened by the Mayor, Thomas North, which had an extensive library, classrooms, a museum and a hall that could seat 800 people. In 1858 Charles Dickens read extracts from his *Christmas Carol* to a capacity audience who had gathered to see a 'live author'. An enlarged Institute building was opened, on the same site, in 1869, the earlier hall having been seriously damaged by fire.

112.   University College in its early days. Opened in 1881, the College owed its existence to the work of the Mechanics' Institute and a local campaign for higher education. It was built of Ancaster stone in a Gothic style popular with Victorian municipal bodies. On first opening it had 381 day students, 623 evening students and 346 students enrolled on government science classes. D.H. Lawrence attended classes at the College between 1906 and 1908.

113.   Opening ceremony of Nottingham University, Highfields, on 10 July 1928. The ceremony was conducted by King George V and Queen Mary, seen here walking through the Central Court of the new University buildings.

114. University Boulevard and the new University buildings in 1932. In 1920 Jesse Boot put forward
a bold scheme for the development of his Highfields Estate. Included in the scheme was a pleasure park,
swimming bath, lake, gardens, university campus and a boulevard which would link Nottingham and
Beeston, running alongside Highfields. In less than 10 years his dream became a reality.

115. Nottingham's Central Reference Library, August 1933. Before moving to its Angel Row site the City Library was
on South Sherwood Street, sharing the University College building. During 1932-3 the library was extended and
refurbished, and a new lighting system was installed.

On The Roads

116. St Peter's Gate, c.1895. Regular horse tram services by Nottingham & District Tramways linked St Peter's with the Midland Station and Great Northern Station, both on the south side of the town. These routes had been introduced in September 1878 and were the first to be opened by the Tramways Company. In 1897 the Company was taken over by Nottingham Corporation.

117. A Bamford horse bus crossing Trent Bridge, 1906. For some years after the introduction of electric trams, horse bus services continued to operate, providing additional routes or supplementing existing ones.

118. An electric tram at Milton's Head corner, May 1902. Decorations have been put up to celebrate the coronation of Edward VII. On 6 January 1890 a petition to the Corporation had complained that 'the tram service in Nottingham is not equal to the requirements of the town. That from the hilly nature of the town, travelling by means of horses is exceedingly slow and expensive, and a quicker and cheaper mode of transit ought to be adopted!' Work on electrification began in 1897 and the first electric tram services were introduced in 1901.

119. Tram conductress Donnelly, one of the first women employed by the Nottingham City Transport Department. She started on 20 September 1915.

120. A motor bus on Parliament Street, opposite the Parliament Street Picture House, c.1927. The service ran between Nottingham, Cinderhill, Bulwell and Hucknall.

YOUR
LUXURY
CARS

USE THEM
for
Business
and
Pleasure

THE
NOTTINGHAM
CITY TRANSPORT

121. In 1927 Nottingham Corporation acquired powers to convert certain tramway routes to trolley-bus operations and experiments began with the use of 'heavy-oil' engined buses. By 1938-39, the year this advertisement appeared, the Corporation had 167 heavy-oil buses, 125 trolley-buses and 50 petrol buses and these vehicles ran over approximately 10,500,000 miles in the year.

122. Before motorised fire engines the Corporation relied on horse-drawn vehicles. Here, a demonstration by the Nottingham fire brigade takes place in front of the Exchange, May 1906.

123. A grand line-up of motor cars outside the Atkey Company salesrooms on Trent Street, 1904. Atkey's was a successful car sales and repair business, with garages and depots both in Nottingham and other Midland towns. Albert Reuben Atkey, who founded the company in 1897, was himself an enthusiastic motorist, going on regular outings with the Nottingham & District Automobile Club.

124. One of Nottingham's earliest recorded car accidents, 1904. Albert Atkey himself probably took the photograph, also noting that: 'We are summoned to Mansfield Road, where an argument had been taking place between an Electric Tram & Mr. A.E. Houfton's 12 H.P. Sunbeam. The Tram Won!'

Waterways & Trent Bridge

125.   Nottingham Canal in 1929, between Wilford Road and Carrington Street, with the Trent Navigation Company warehouse towering above. Despite the presence of railways, the canal was still a busy waterway.

126.   The old and new Trent Bridges stand side by side in 1871. The old bridge had become increasingly unsafe, especially during flood periods, and in 1869 the foundation stone for a new bridge was laid by John Barber, mayor of Nottingham. On 25 July 1871 the new Trent Bridge was opened and the old one was subsequently demolished.

127. Construction work on Holme Lock, May 1922. Holme Lock was one of a series of locks and weirs built on the Trent between Nottingham and Newark, which converted this stretch of the river into a modern waterway.

128. A view over Trent Bridge and West Bridgford in 1900. As Nottingham expanded and communications to the south improved over Trent Bridge, the suburb of West Bridgford grew rapidly. In 1851 its population was only 250 but by 1901 it had grown to more than 7,000.

129. Trent Bridge Water Works were designed by Thomas Hawksley, an engineer who later practised in London, gaining a national reputation for his engineering skill. The Trent Bridge Works opened in 1831, using Trent river water that had been filtered through brick tunnels set in natural beds of sand and gravel. For a time Hawksley himself lived at the Works.

Railways

130.   Nottingham's first railway line was opened by the Midland Counties Railway in May 1839, linking Derby and Nottingham, with later connections to Rugby and London. A Grecian-style station fronted Queen's Road and acted as the line's terminus until 1848. In 1839 the first class fare to Derby was 3s. 6d. and second class was 2s.

131.   Interior of the second Midland Station, opened in 1848. It stood on the present station site but passengers used an entrance on Station Street itself. The new station had become necessary with the opening of a new line to Lincoln on 4 August 1846. The old Queen's Road terminus was demolished.

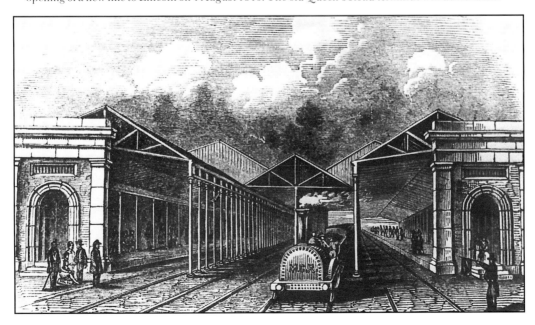

132. Nottingham's third Midland Station in the 1930s. Moves towards the construction of a new Midland Station were largely inspired by the opening of the Victoria Station in 1900, a rival both for traffic and status. The Midland was built in Edwardian style by A.E. Lambert, its main entrance façade standing on Carrington Street Bridge. It was opened on 17 January 1904.

133. Looking towards the present Midland Station from Wilford Road. The railway lines are almost submerged by flood water.

WHITSUNTIDE IN LONDON.

Messrs. STEVENSON Ltd. have arranged with the Midland Railway Co.
to run

On SATURDAY, June 2nd, 1900

AN EMPLOYES' EXCURSION TRAIN TO

LONDON

(ST. PANCRAS)

AT A FARE OF 4/-

From Hucknall	6-50 a.m.	
„ Bulwell	6-55 „	The Return Train
„ Basford	7-0 „	will leave
„ Radford	7-5 „	St. Pancras Station
„ Lenton	7-10 „	at 12-20 midnight
„ NOTTINGHAM	7-20 „	same day.

Passengers can stay in London up to Saturday, June 9th, by presenting their Tickets at the Booking Office, St. Pancras Station, and paying for return on Sunday, June 3rd, at 3-15 p.m. and 12-0 midnight, **1s.** ; and on other days at 9-0 a.m., and 12-25, 3-0, 4-55 p.m. and 12-0 midnight, **2s.**

TICKETS can be obtained at the Works of STEVENSON LTD., Davis Street, Carlton Road; from H. HOLMES, 27, St. Ann's Well Road; H. F. KERSHAW, 99, Woodborough Road; J. T. RADFORD, Mechanics' Institute; J. ROBINSON, 16, Burton Street; BAINES BROS., 41, Broad Street; C. WOOLAND'S, 148, Arkwright Street; J. GRIMM, 19, Broad Marsh; Mrs. GOULDER, 7, Willoughby Street, Lenton; F. CLARK, 36, Radford Road; Mr. LOVERSEED, 8, Ekowe Street, Basford; Mr. BARNES, Market Place, Bulwell; Mrs. HOLROYD, Hucknall Torkard; also from

T. HODKINSON, 86, Alfreton Road, to whom all applications must be made for Engaged Compartments.

☞ The number of Tickets is strictly limited, and must be obtained not later than Thursday, May 31st.

Accident Assurance Tickets can be obtained at Cook's Excursion Offices, 16, Clumber Street, and 97, Derby Road.

N.B.—121/1000 (C)

134.   Railway excursions were popular from the beginning of the railway era. This Midland Railway employees' excursion on 2 June 1900 started at Hucknall at 6.50 a.m., and returned from St Pancras at 12.20; the fare was 4 shillings.

135. Two railway navvies working on the Great Central railway line make the best of an old cellar of the Nottingham
Union Workhouse, 1897. The Great Central was one of the last main lines to be built in the country.

136. Bulwell viaduct under construction in about 1898. This photograph leaves no doubt as to the enormous scale of work involved in major railway undertakings. Bulwell viaduct was part of a Manchester, Sheffield & Lincolnshire railway line (later the Great Central) extended from Sheffield, down through Nottinghamshire, then on to London and the South.

137. Navvy Mission Room, Main Street, Bulwell, 1897, opened to attend the spiritual needs of the navvies working on the Manchester, Sheffield and Lincolnshire railway. The missionary looks down from the raised platform over the rows of hard benches.

138. The Victoria Station and, on the right, Hotel, c.1910. Originally it was known either as the Nottingham Joint Station (the name used by the Great Northern) or Nottingham Central (by the Great Central), as it was shared by the two companies. However, a compromise was eventually achieved when it was suggested the station be named after Queen Victoria as it was opened on her birthday, 24 May 1900. Construction work involved the demolition of no less than 1,300 houses, the Nottingham Union Workhouse and numerous local streets. In 1967 the station was demolished to make way for the Victoria Shopping Centre, though the clock tower remains as a monument to the great age of steam.

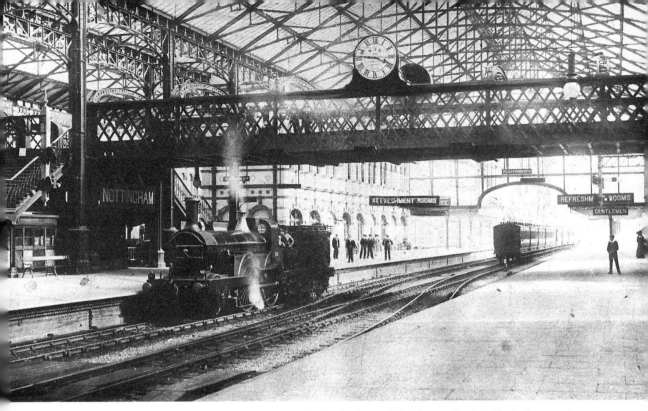

139. A Stirling 2-4-0 locomotive at Nottingham's Victoria Station in about 1910. That station had 12 platforms and seven ticket-issuing windows, three each for the Great Central and Great Northern and one for excursion tickets.

140. St Ann's Well Station c.1904, one of a series of stations on the Suburban line that linked Nottingham with the expanding suburbs of St Ann's, Sneinton, Mapperley and Sherwood. Its short 3½-mile length involved the construction of 15 bridges, five tunnels, three stations and substantial earthworks. The line was opened in 1889.

Housing

141. A rather romanticised impression of Nottingham from the south, showing some of the Park's handsome villa residences. Originally a deer park for Nottingham Castle, the Park was developed as a prestigious residential estate in the 19th century by the Dukes of Newcastle. The Castle had been rebuilt as a private residence for the first Duke of Newcastle in 1674-9, and after being burned down in 1831 was restored as a Public Museum and Art Gallery in 1876-8. Many of the Park's street names reflect the area's long association with the Newcastle family. Building in the Park began in the 1820s and continued until the end of the century. About 200 of its 650 houses were built by Thomas Chambers Hine, a distinguished local architect who was engaged as the Newcastle estate's surveyor in 1854.

142. Thomas Chambers Hine (1813-99) in the conservatory of his house, 25 Regent Street, which he himself designed. Other than houses in the Park, his buildings include the Adams & Page warehouse, the Corn Exchange, All Saints' church, the Great Northern Station on London Road and the Coppice Hospital.

143. Plans for two semi-detached villas on Sherwood Rise by Watson Fothergill, submitted for approval to the Corporation's Planning Committee in March 1894. Fothergill's unique blend of style, design and materials can be seen in buildings all over Nottingham. They include prestigious villas, terraced housing, large department stores, individual shops and offices, multistorey warehouses, and banks. All were designed not only with flair and imagination, but also with painstaking care over every detail.

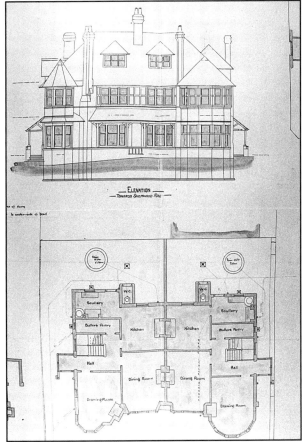

144. Houses in Narrow Marsh, 1913. Many of these houses would have originally been occupied by framework knitters, the top-storey windows being extended to allow in as much light as possible to help in the operation of the frames. However, by 1913 many of them had become unsuitable for habitation and the City Council began a major demolition programme in the area.

145. A photograph of Parr's Yard, Page Street, taken in 1931, some time before it was demolished by the City Council. These sunless and enclosed courts had been built in the 19th century, many by unscrupulous builders, and they frequentl lacked modern sanitary facilities.

146. New housing by Nottingham Corporation advances over Colwick Hill in 1932. This view of the Colwick Hill Estate is taken from Overdale Road and looks down Ashdale Road. A lorry delivering coal from the Bestwood Iron & Coal Company is stuck in the mud.

Around & About

147. Thatched cottages on Main Road, Wilford, *c*.1906. Although Wilford lay only a short distance from Nottingham, the village retained its picturesque rural charm for many years and it was much visited by trippers and cyclists.

148. Clifton Grove boasted one of the finest avenues of trees in the Midlands. Its elms had been planted in 1690 by Sir Gervas Clifton to grace the carriage drive from the river bank to Clifton Hall, but it also became a favourite walk and picnic spot for 'thousands of Nottingham artisans with their wives and families, young men and maidens'. Unfortunately the Grove's mighty elms fell victim to the ravages of Dutch Elm Disease.

149. Led by a local band, a Sunday parade makes its way along Main Street, Bulwell, c.1904.
Bulwell grew rapidly in the 19th and early 20th centuries. A large proportion of the working
population was employed in surrounding coal mines and others worked in local quarries,
brickyards, lime kilns, hosiery mills and in the bleaching industry. The growing community was
served by a diverse range of religious organisations.

150. A view from the south over the Meadows, c.1901. Before the 1845 Enclosure Act the Meadows was one of
Nottingham's great open-fields, stretching from the River Trent up to the town. It was renowned for its annual
bloom of crocuses, commemorated in the name Crocus Street. On the right is London Road, originally known as the
Flood Road because it was constructed on a causeway to raise it above flood level, and to the left is Arkwright Street.
The area was built up rapidly after Enclosure, though much of the original housing was cleared and replaced in the
1970s.

151. The district of St Ann's takes its name from St Ann's Well, shown here in the 1870s. Its ornamental cover dates from 1857 when the Council allowed a sum of £100 for its construction. In August 1887 it was demolished to make way for an embankment of the Suburban Railway. Until modern times St Ann's was fields, coppices and open land, and during the summer visitors to the well would play bowls, listen to musical concerts or pass the time in a nearby tavern.

152. J.L. Huskinson, chemist and dentist of Commercial Square, St Ann's, 1875. In the front window are advertisements for Dr. Rooke's Oriental Pills and Mrs. Herbert's American Hair Dressing. The site was later occupied by the Westminster Bank, at the corner of Union Road and Alfred Street Central.

153.   Sneinton Market, 1931. Until the 19th century Sneinton was a rural village lying at the edge of Nottingham. Then, as industry and housing spread, the two places grew together, and in 1877 Sneinton joined Nottingham under the Extension Act. The market, however, was in existence even before 1877. Behind the market stands the Ragged School.

154. Rock dwellings at Sneinton Hermitage. On visiting these 'dens and caves' in the 18th century, John Throsby had been astonished to see people 'inhabiting the very bowels of the earth'. The rock houses were inhabited by people up until 1867, and until the 1890s two public houses remained which had been built into the cliff face. Between 1897 and 1919 the buildings were demolished during railway construction work.

155. Mansfield Road, Sherwood, c.1920, with two trams crossing near the Corporation tram depot, just visible on the left. Sherwood and Nottingham were linked by an electric tram service from January 1901, when the fare to the Market Square was 2d. The new tram services contributed towards Sherwood's rapid growth in the early 20th century.

Nottingham at War

156.   A detachment of Robin Hood Rifles have set off from the Drill Hall on the first stage of their long journey to France.

The
GREAT·WAR
THE STANDARD HISTORY OF THE ALL-EUROPE CONFLICT
Edited by H.W.Wilson, author of
"With the Flag to Pretoria", "Japan's Fight for Freedom", etc.

157.   Front cover of *The Great War* magazine, 17 February 1917, showing air ace Albert Ball. One of the war's most successful pilots, Albert Ball shot down over 40 enemy aircraft and one air balloon. He died in 1917 when his aircraft came down in France behind enemy lines. He was buried by the Germans with full military honours and was awarded a posthumous Victoria Cross.

158.   Zeppelin raids caused extensive damage in some parts of Nottingham. On
23 September 1916 a raid completely destroyed several houses in Newthorpe Street, in the
Meadows. A resident of the Meadows wrote: 'Nearly every shop from here to the Market
Place has broken windows. Two houses were demolished in Newthorpe Street. They were
searching for bodies when we went out'.

159.   Women at the Raleigh Cycle Company making shell fuses during the First World War. At the beginning of the war
Raleigh changed from manufacturing cycles to the production of small munitions, with women providing most of the
labour force.

160. A Nottingham policeman lends a helping hand to evacuees the Central Bus Station. In total around 5,000 people were evacuated from Nottingham during the Second World War, some to villages and towns in Nottinghamshire, some to other counties. Evacuations and a whole range of air raid precautions were the responsibility of a special Emergency Committee.

161. Youngsters in the Air Training Corps boarding a Skill's bus, possibly setting off on a training exercise. Judging from the expressions on their faces, they have mixed feelings about the day ahead.

162.   Women air raid wardens inspect gas masks in 1940, one of many tasks performed by women during World War Two. As well as their involvement in air raid precautions, women helped to run postal services, worked in munitions, on farms around Nottingham, and kept local transport services going.

RATIONING
of Clothing, Cloth, Footwear
from June 1, 1941

Rationing has been introduced, not to deprive you of your real needs, but to make more certain that you get your share of the country's goods—to get fair shares with everybody else.

When the shops re-open you will be able to buy cloth, clothes, footwear and knitting wool *only if you bring your Food Ration Book with you.* The shopkeeper will detach the required number of coupons from the unused margarine page. Each margarine coupon counts as one coupon towards the purchase of clothing or footwear. You will have a total of 66 coupons to last you for a year; so go sparingly. You can buy *where* you like and *when* you like without registering.

NUMBER OF COUPONS NEEDED

Men and Boys	Adult	Child	Women and Girls	Adult	Child
Unlined mackintosh or cape ..	9	7	Lined mackintoshes, or coats (over 28 in. in length) ..	14	11
Other mackintoshes, or raincoat, or overcoat	16	11	Jacket, or short coat (under 28 in. in length)	11	8
Coat, or jacket, or blazer or like garment	13	8	Dress, or gown, or frock—woollen	11	8
Waistcoat, or pull-over, or cardigan, or jersey ..	5	3	Dress, or gown, or frock—other material	7	5
Trousers (other than fustian or corduroy)	8	6	Gym tunic, or girl's skirt with bodice	8	6
Fustian or corduroy trousers ..	5	5	Blouse, or sports shirt, or cardigan, or jumper	5	3
Shorts	5	3	Skirt, or divided skirt ..	7	5
Overalls, or dungarees or like garment	6	4	Overalls, or dungarees or like garment	6	4
Dressing-gown or bathing-gown	8	6	Apron, or pinafore	3	2
Night-shirt or pair of pyjamas ..	8	6	Pyjamas	8	6
Shirt, or combinations—woollen	8	6	Nightdress	6	5
Shirt, or combinations—other material	5	4	Petticoat, or slip, or combination, or cami-knickers	4	3
Pants, or vest, or bathing costume, or child's blouse	4	2	Other undergarments, including corsets	3	2
Pair of socks or stockings ..	3	1	Pair of stockings	2	1
Collar, or tie, or pair of cuffs ..	1	1	Pair of socks (ankle length) ..	1	1
Two handkerchiefs	1	1	Collar, or tie, or pair of cuffs ..	1	1
Scarf, or pair of gloves or mittens	2	2	Two handkerchiefs	1	1
Pair of slippers or goloshes ..	4	2	Scarf, or pair of gloves or mittens or muff	2	2
Pair of boots or shoes ..	7	3	Pair of slippers, boots or shoes ..	5	3
Pair of leggings, gaiters or spats	3	2			

CLOTH. Coupons needed per yard depend on the width. For example, a yard of woollen cloth 36 inches wide requires 3 coupons. The same amount of cotton or other cloth needs 2 coupons.
KNITTING WOOL. 1 coupon for two ounces.

THESE GOODS MAY BE BOUGHT *WITHOUT* COUPONS

¶ Children's clothing of sizes generally suitable for infants less than 4 years old. ¶ Boiler suits and workmen's bib and brace overalls. ¶ Hats and caps. ¶ Sewing thread. ¶ Mending wool and mending silk. ¶ Boot and shoe laces. ¶ Tapes, braids, ribbons and other fabrics of 3 inches or less in width. ¶ Elastic. ¶ Lace and lace net. ¶ Sanitary towels. ¶ Braces, suspenders and garters. ¶ Hard haberdashery. ¶ Clogs. ¶ Black-out cloth dyed black. ¶ All second-hand articles.

Special Notice to Retailers

Retailers will be allowed to get fresh stocks of cloth up to and including June 28th, of other rationed goods up to and including June 21st, WITHOUT SURRENDERING COUPONS. After those dates they will be able to obtain fresh stocks only by turning in their customers' coupons. Steps have been taken, in the interests of the smaller retailers, to limit during these periods the quantity of goods which can be supplied by a wholesaler or manufacturer to any one retailer however large his orders. *Further information can be obtained from your Trade Organisations.*

ISSUED BY THE BOARD OF TRADE

163. Board of Trade notice issued to help shoppers and retailers with the rationing of clothing, cloth and footwear from 1 June 1941. Guidance was given on the number of coupons needed for particular items.

164. Bomb damage on Friar Lane following a raid on the night of 8-9 May 1941. During the raid nearly 500 high-explosive bombs were dropped on the city as well as thousands of incendiaries. Two hundred people were killed and hundreds more were injured. Nineteen factories, offices and warehouses were destroyed, 60 houses and shops, two schools and 34 public buildings. Although Nottingham had 228 air raids during the war, that night in May was the most intense. It became known as the 'Night of The Blitz'.

165. During the blitz of 8-9 May 1941 University College, Shakespeare Street, received a direct hit. Other public buildings hit that night included the Old Moot Hall, the Masonic Hall and the Registry Office on Shakespeare Street.